W9-CNA-370

# EQUALITY
## IN SPORTS

BY TRACY MILLER

Show Racism the Red Card

Show Racism the Red Card

Printed in the United States of America,
North Mankato, Minnesota
102013
012014

 THIS BOOK CONTAINS AT LEAST 10% RECYCLED MATERIALS.

Editor: Chrös McDougall
Series Designer: Craig Hinton

**Photo credits:** Lynne Cameron/Press Association via AP Images, cover, 1; AP Images, 5, 17, 18, 21, 54; Dave Martin/AP Images, 8; Rob Carmell/Cal Sport Media via AP Images, 12; Stew Milne/ AP Images, 15; Anthony Nesmith/Cal Sport Media via AP Images, 24; Antonio Calanni/AP Images, 27; Kevork Djansezian/AP Images, 29; Eric Risber/AP Images, 32; Feliz Kaestle/DAPD/AP Images, 36; Cal Sport Media via AP Images, 38; Bettmann/Corbis, 41; Walter Attenni/AP Images, 43; Kirsty Wigglesworth/AP Images, 49; Duane Burleson/AP Images, 51; Eric Gay/AP Images, 56; Rick Friedman/rickfriedman.com/Corbis, 59

Library of Congress Control Number: 2013946561

**Cataloging-in-Publication Data**

Miller, Tracy.
 Equality in sports / Tracy Miller.
  p. cm. -- (Issues in sports)
Includes bibliographical references and index.
ISBN 978-1-62403-121-2
1. Sports--Moral and ethical aspects--Juvenile literature.  2. Racism in sports--Juvenile literature.
3. Sex discrimination in sports--Juvenile literature.   I. Title.
796--dc23

                                    2013946561


**Content Consultant:** B. David Ridpath, Ed. D.
Associate Professor and Kahandas Nandola Professor of Sports Administration
Ohio University, College of Business

# TABLE OF CONTENTS

## Chapter 1
The Right to Play     4

## Chapter 2
The Fight against Racism     16

## Chapter 3
No Girls Allowed     28

## Chapter 4
Overcoming Disabilities     40

## Chapter 5
Coming Out     50

Discussion Questions     60

Glossary     61

For More information     62

Index     64

About the Author     64

Tennis player Arthur Ashe fought for equality in sports and in society during his lifetime. ▶

# THE RIGHT TO PLAY

A nyone can play sports. Right? Well, not exactly. For years, many people have had to fight for the right to play. Many have not been allowed to compete because other people said they had to play separately or not play at all. People have had to fight for equality in society. They have also had to fight for equality in sports.

Arthur Ashe never took the easy route in his push for equality. Growing up in the 1950s in Richmond, Virginia, Ashe decided to play tennis. Tennis was played mostly by white people at the time. Ashe was black, but that never stopped him. He was not always welcome at tournaments. People sometimes treated him poorly because of his skin

color. But he showed up and always acted civil. Ashe knew some people in the tennis community looked down on him. They believed that black people were inferior and did not belong in the mostly white, upper-class sport. Many of those people were looking for a reason to kick Ashe out. But he never gave them one.

Ashe continued to find success in tennis. He earned a scholarship to play tennis in college. Later he won three Grand Slam titles. But Ashe is remembered more for being a leader than for his success on the court. He was a pioneer in tennis. Ashe treated people with respect while standing up for his beliefs. That helped the tennis community become more accepting of black players. His efforts helped open the sport to a new generation of black players, such as Serena and Venus Williams.

Ashe often used his fame to push for equality in all areas of life. He paid special attention to South Africa. That country had adopted a policy of segregation called apartheid in the 1940s. The white minority there severely discriminated against blacks and other racial groups. Nonwhites could not live in the same areas or use the same public facilities as whites. Nonwhites also were not allowed to represent the country in athletics, including in the Olympic Games. Many international sports organizations barred South Africa from participating due to this policy.

In 1973, Ashe traveled to South Africa. He met with locals and played in a tennis tournament. He hoped to not only raise international awareness of apartheid but also to serve as an inspiration to black South

Africans. South Africa finally began undoing its discriminatory laws in the early 1990s. The country still suffers from extreme racial inequality. But many parts of South African life, including its national sports teams, are now open to people of all races. And South Africa is now welcome to compete in the Olympics and other international sporting events.

Ashe died from acquired immunodeficiency syndrome (AIDS) in 1993. The former tennis star had gotten the virus that leads to AIDS during a medical procedure. It could have happened to anybody. Ashe spent his final months raising awareness about the virus. His efforts helped show many people that AIDS affects everyone and needed attention. Ashe's public battle with AIDS helped others better understand and better accept those who suffered from it.

Ashe's battles for equality in sports and in the world were not forgotten. In the fall of 1992, *Sports Illustrated* named Ashe its Sportsman of the Year. In 1993, ESPN created an annual award show called the Excellence in Sports Performance Yearly, or ESPYS. One of the highest honors each year is the Arthur Ashe Courage Award. The award goes to people who "reflect the spirit of Arthur Ashe, possessing strength in the

## ISOLATED

First it was the International Olympic Committee (IOC). Then it was soccer's international governing body. In 1964, both organizations banned South Africa. The country could not send a team to the 1964 Olympic Games in Tokyo, Japan. South Africa would not be eligible for the 1966 World Cup in England, either. The moves sent a powerful message about equality in sports. The IOC demanded that South Africa give equal opportunities in sports to whites and nonwhites. It also wanted the country to publicly condemn racial discrimination in sports. South Africa refused. As such, no South African competed in the Olympic Games or World Cup until after the apartheid laws ended in 1991.

face of adversity, courage in the face of peril, and the willingness to stand up for their beliefs no matter what the cost." Ashe was just one of many people in the sports community who worked to make their games—and the world—more inclusive. But the work continues.

## RACISM

Throughout history, people have held prejudices about those who have different characteristics. Those characteristics include things such as people's skin color, birthplace, language, nationality, or religion. Sometimes one group oppresses or discriminates against another based on these characteristics. That is called racism. It exists in both subtle and obvious forms.

Racism exists in many parts of life. In the United States, racism against blacks has existed for centuries. Whites were allowed to own black people as slaves until 1865. But even after that, racism remained a part of the culture and laws. Blacks were segregated and discriminated against. They were not allowed to attend the same schools or public facilities as whites. Businesses, including sports teams, could refuse to hire or serve somebody because of the person's skin color.

That is no longer the case. The United States passed laws to end racial discrimination and segregation during the 1950s and 1960s. These changes were part of the civil rights movement. Sports played a major role in this transition, especially baseball.

Sports leagues can no longer ban certain races. Racism has not gone away, though. Some people still believe their race to be superior. This sometimes comes out in the form of racist insults or chants at sporting events. Racial stereotypes persist, too. For example, coaches sometimes prefer white quarterbacks and black running backs in football. Still, racism in sports is not as obvious as it once was. And many people are working to make sure racism in sports is soon a thing of the past.

## SEXISM

Sexism is another form of inequality. It occurs when people discriminate against others based on their sex. Traditionally, sexism has most often occurred against women. In the United States, women were not allowed to vote until 1920. They are still fighting for equality in other ways. And the fight extends to sports.

Sexism has had a long history in sports. Many modern sports were founded or first organized during the 1800s. But most of the sports were limited to men. Physical activity was seen as improper and even harmful for women. Sometimes women were banned from competing in sports altogether. Sometimes they were allowed to compete only in modified versions of men's sports. Opportunities did exist for female athletes. However, they were almost always limited.

Women have battled for equal opportunities in sports throughout the twentieth century. The battle has sometimes been slow. But the gains have been huge. Today most countries allow women to compete in all sports. In the United States, schools are required to fund women's and men's sports equally.

Problems remain, however. Some countries still ban women's sports. In many countries, women's sports do not receive the same level of support as men's sports. But female athletes continue to challenge these attitudes. They now compete at the highest levels, including the Olympic Games. And they are showing that women can be amazing athletes, just like men.

# LGBT RIGHTS

The lesbian, gay, bisexual, and transgender (LGBT) community is also fighting for equal rights. For years people have been discriminated against because of their sexual orientation or gender identity. Still today LGBT individuals are targets of abuse. Some people believe it is not okay to be an LGBT person. But the LGBT community is working to change that. Their battle exists in society as well as sports.

Throughout the world, laws target LGBT people or limit their freedom. Opinions have begun to change, though. This is especially true in the United States. Some states and institutions have taken steps to protect the rights of LGBT people. But these laws and policies are not universal. And some parts of the country remain hostile toward LGBT people.

Many LGBT athletes feel the need to hide their sexual identities. There are many possible reasons for this. The athletes might believe "coming out" could lead to discrimination. This could include fewer opportunities for jobs or endorsements. LGBT athletes also might fear abuse from teammates and fans. Nobody can say for sure how an athlete would be received upon coming out. But in the past, the reception has often been negative.

However, anti-LGBT attitudes appear to be changing. Some sports leagues and teams have publicly supported LGBT equality. National

## MLS'S FIRST OPENLY GAY PLAYER

On May 27, 2013, *USA TODAY* reported a first. Robbie Rogers became the first openly gay player in Major League Soccer (MLS). "I guess this is a historic thing, but for me it was just a soccer game," Rogers said. Rogers had initially retired from soccer after making his sexual orientation public in February 2013. The 26-year-old made the announcement on his blog while playing for a team in England. But his retirement did not last long. Rogers missed playing soccer. By May 2013 he was back on the field with a new team, the Los Angeles Galaxy.

Basketball Association (NBA) star Kobe Bryant used an antigay slur during a 2011 game. The league fined him $100,000. MLS went a step further in 2013. The league suspended player Alan Gordon for three games for using an antigay slur. The incidents showed that antigay slurs are still an issue in sports. But the reactions showed how leagues are cracking down on that kind of abuse.

Later in 2013, an NBA player and an MLS player came out as gay. Several athletes had come out before them. But the two athletes in 2013 proved significant. They were the first active players in major US men's professional sports leagues to come out. And media and fans largely applauded their announcements. Others were more cautious in celebrating, though. They pointed out that these were the first two players to come out. It is believed more LGBT players remain wary of doing so.

## DISABILITY DISCRIMINATION

Disability discrimination occurs when someone is treated unequally due to a physical or mental disability. For many years, people with disabilities were treated as second-class citizens. They were not given opportunities equal to their nondisabled peers. This was true in school, in the workplace, and in sports. This trend is changing. Many people are pushing for equal rights and opportunities for people with disabilities. And sports are playing a major role in the movement.

For years a wheelchair was seen as a crutch. Most people who needed wheelchairs could not walk. So those people were often treated as less important than nondisabled people. That perception is changing. People like Josh Cassidy are showing that a wheelchair does not have to hold them back. Instead, it can be sports equipment.

As a baby, Cassidy was diagnosed with cancer in his spine. He overcame the cancer. However, his legs were paralyzed. That never stopped him, though. Cassidy is now one of the fastest wheelchair racers in the world. In 2012, he set a new world record in winning the Boston Marathon men's wheelchair race.

"Paralympic or Olympic?" he asks on his Web site. "Call it what you want. I'm an athlete."

Cassidy is one of many who view themselves as athletes more than as people with disabilities. These athletes are as competitive as any other athlete. And they are changing people's perceptions about disabilities.

Many organizations are helping provide opportunities for athletes with disabilities. The International Paralympic Committee (IPC) organizes the Paralympic Games. The Paralympics showcase the world's greatest athletes with disabilities on a major stage. But disabled sports are making an impact on all levels. US Paralympics oversees disabled sports in the United States. It works with world-class athletes. But US Paralympics

Josh Cassidy of Canada adjusts his wheelchair ▲
prior to the 2013 Boston Marathon.

also works on the grassroots level to introduce people with disabilities
to sports.

Sports have also shown to be a great tool for rehabilitation. The
Warrior Games is a series of competitions for wounded military veterans.
Many of the veterans have lost limbs or have other disabilities. But they
never lost their competitive drive. Competing helps them recover.

## CHAPTER 2

Jackie Robinson broke baseball's color line in 1947 and helped the United States become more open to racial equality. ▶

# THE FIGHT AGAINST RACISM

B ranch Rickey was the general manager of the Brooklyn Dodgers. And in the mid-1940s, he was ready to sign a black player. That player would be the first black player in the modern major leagues. So Rickey knew how important it was to get the *right* player.

Both baseball and the United States were largely segregated at the time. Blacks did not have the same rights as whites. In parts of the country blacks could not go to the same schools or even use the same drinking fountains as whites. They even faced hatred. Some white people believed blacks were inferior. These whites were not interested in integration. And some would use verbal or physical abuse to make their point.

Baseball, meanwhile, was by far the most popular sport in the United States. What happened in baseball was a big deal. So the player Rickey signed would have to stay calm while being abused and discriminated against. And the player would also have to be able to handle pressure. After all, the signing would be historic. And if it worked, baseball could help lead the United States toward integration. Rickey found the right man in Jackie Robinson.

## DRAWING THE COLOR LINE

Baseball had a long and rich history in the United States. It was founded sometime during the early 1800s. And it became very popular after the Civil War ended in 1865. People across the country wanted to play. And many did play—black and white. Sometimes they even played together.

But race relations at the time were tense. Black players were sometimes taunted and threatened by white fans and players. The racism was especially strong in the South, where slavery had existed until 1865. Nonetheless, in 1878 Bud Fowler made history. He was the first black player to join a white professional team. More black players followed.

Then black players started to disappear from organized baseball. Organized baseball refers to the major leagues and affiliated minor leagues. The first World Series was in 1903. By then, no blacks remained in organized baseball.

There was no official rule barring black players. It was an unwritten rule. Some white players and officials had pressured teams to stop signing black players. Eventually all of the teams followed. The divide became known as the color line. No black player crossed it for decades.

## BASEBALL'S DIVIDE

The rest of society was similarly divided. Blacks could no longer be owned as slaves. That did not mean they had equal rights, though. Black people could legally be denied service at restaurants due to

### JESSE OWENS

Racism was a major story at the 1936 Olympic Games in Berlin, Germany. German chancellor Adolf Hitler hoped to use the Games to promote his racist views. Hitler believed the so-called Aryan race—which the Nazis generally identified by blond hair, blue eyes, and white skin—was the most pure and thus better than the rest. Others, such as blacks and Jews, were discriminated against. However, the star of that year's Games was a black American named Jesse Owens. Owens won four gold medals in track and field. He became an American hero. And in the process he became a symbol that Hitler's racist views were wrong. However, Owens returned home to a still-segregated United States. He worked to promote racial equality but at times struggled to find stable work.

their skin color. Hotels could refuse to house them. And then there was segregation. Blacks could go to school. But in parts of the country, they could not go to the same schools as white kids.

Baseball followed a similar path. Blacks could not play in the major leagues. But they still wanted to play. So they formed all-black leagues. These were called the Negro Leagues.

The Negro Leagues had rich histories. Most historians agree that the best black players of the time would have thrived in the majors, too. But they never had that opportunity. The segregation laws in the United States were known as "separate but equal." But they were usually not equal. The white facilities were usually higher quality. That was the case with baseball, too. The Negro Leagues had some great players. But the all-black leagues were in the shadow of the major leagues. Many teams lost money. Teams constantly went out of business. Facilities were often run down. It was a constant struggle for these leagues to survive.

Society's views about racial discrimination were changing by the 1940s, however. The United States was involved in World War II from 1941 to 1945. Many black soldiers had fought and died for the United States. This made people wonder why blacks could die for their country but not play in the major leagues.

That was where Rickey stepped in. He saw an opportunity to use sports to help lead the country toward racial integration. To be sure, Rickey had practical reasons, too. He knew there were many great black

Jackie Robinson, *right*, signs a contract to join the ▲
Brooklyn Dodgers' minor league team in 1945.

ball players. He also knew he could probably get a really good black player
for a good price. But Rickey was certainly aware of the significance. That is
why he needed to make sure he picked the right player.

"I don't think you can help but feel that if the Robinson experiment
failed, it would have pushed the notion of integrating sports—but also
integrating other aspects of business life in our society—probably back,"
said Bob Kendrick, the Negro Leagues Baseball Museum marketing
director, in 2008. "That's why this thing is so relevant, because failure was
not an option."

# STRAIGHT TO THE SOURCE

The Brooklyn Dodgers opened the 1947 season on April 15 at Ebbets Field. Starting at first base for the Dodgers was rookie Jackie Robinson. That morning, *New York Times* writer Arthur Daley commented on the Dodgers' attempts to play down the attention on Robinson in his major league debut:

> *It is merely an attempt to lighten the pressure on Robinson's shoulders. In like fashion the Mahatma waited until the Montreal Royals were in Panama before he ordered that Jackie be switched to first base. Yet nothing can actually lighten the pressure, and [Robinson] realizes it full well. There is no way of disguising the fact that he is not an ordinary rookie and no amount of pretense can make it otherwise.*

Source: Daley, Arthur. "Play Ball!" New York Times. *15 April 1947. 31.*

## What's the Big Idea?

Jackie Robinson went on to be an important figure both in baseball and in race relations in the United States. On April 15, 1947, however, nobody knew how things would turn out. What do you think is the writer's main point in this passage? Use evidence to back it up.

Robinson joined the Dodgers' minor league team in 1946. He joined the Dodgers one year later. As Rickey expected, insults and discrimination followed. Fans and players would yell, threaten, and sometimes try to hurt Robinson. But he kept his cool. And he thrived.

Robinson was named the 1947 National League (NL) Rookie of the Year. He was the 1949 NL Most Valuable Player. And his presence on the field was winning over white fans as well as black fans.

## INTEGRATING SPORTS

Robinson was not the first great black athlete to compete with whites. The sprinter Jesse Owens starred at the 1936 Olympic Games. Boxer Joe Louis was also a star in the 1930s. ESPN called Louis "the first African-American to achieve hero worship that was previously reserved for whites only." Even the National Football League (NFL) integrated before baseball. The NFL broke a 14-year trend by welcoming black players back into the league in 1946. None proved to be as significant as Robinson, though.

Baseball's popularity made Robinson a major national story. And as he thrived with the Dodgers, he opened people's eyes. White fans began to cheer for him. Other teams began to sign black players. By the 1950–51 season, the NBA included black players as well. Then the civil rights movement took hold in the 1950s and 1960s. That led to new laws that ended racial discrimination and segregation. Many credit sports— particularly Rickey and Robinson—with helping that movement succeed.

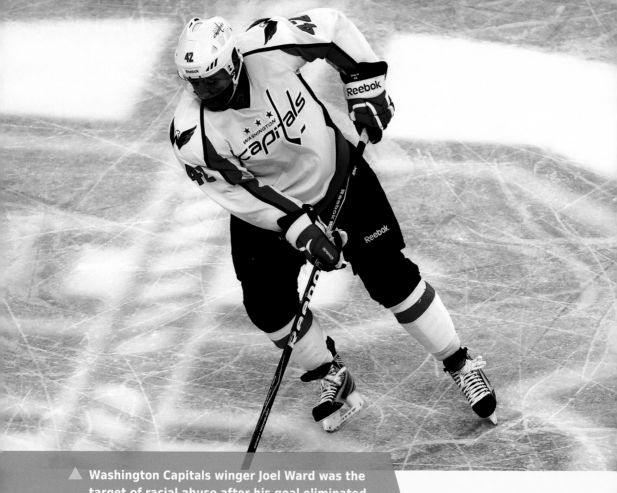

## RACISM TODAY

Sports today are integrated. Racism is uniformly condemned among major sports organizations. However, racist beliefs and behavior still persist. That showed during the 2012 National Hockey League (NHL) playoffs. Washington Capitals wing Joel Ward scored the goal that knocked out the Boston Bruins. As expected, Bruins fans were bummed.

EQUALITY IN SPORTS

Some went on Twitter to share their feelings. And a few of them used racial slurs against Ward, who happens to be black.

Those racist outbursts were troubling. Sports had long been integrated. But the reactions showed that racism was not gone completely. However, the counterreaction to the attacks showed how things had changed. In Robinson's time, those types of public attacks were common and even accepted. In 2012, the Bruins and the NHL both condemned the slurs. The Bruins even issued a public apology. The sports Web site *Deadspin* went a step further. It published the tweets and the usernames for everyone to see. This was meant to publicly shame those who made the comments.

Such direct and public acts of racism are much less common in the United States than they were in 1947. However, public displays of racism remain a major concern in international soccer. The fans of some teams are organized white supremacists. That means they believe whites are better than all other races. Sometimes white fans make

## FIGHTING STEREOTYPES

Direct and public racism is condemned in US sports leagues. However, racial stereotypes still plague sports culture. This is especially common in football. At the highest levels, football teams are often diverse. They have a mix of players of all races and backgrounds. However, coaches and media members sometimes show bias about race and certain positions. This is most common with quarterbacks. Good white players are often labeled as being "smart." Good black quarterbacks are more commonly referred to as being "athletic." *Time* magazine explored these issues in a 2013 profile of biracial quarterback Colin Kaepernick: "Does race explain why dual-threat quarterbacks like [Kaepernick], Robert Griffin III of Washington, and Russell Wilson of Seattle—all black—are more likely to be labeled '[athletic] freaks' than, say, [white quarterback] Andrew Luck of the Indianapolis Colts?" Kaepernick said he wants to break the stereotype. He believes black quarterbacks can be smart and white quarterbacks can be athletic.

Kevin-Prince Boateng, a midfielder for AC Milan ▶
in Italy, wears an antiracism message on his
shirt during a 2013 game.

monkey sounds and throw bananas at black players. Historically, some people have compared blacks to monkeys as a way of discrimination. The taunting is meant to say that blacks are less evolved, or less human, than whites.

Soccer organizations are cracking down on racism. Tough penalties are in place for racist acts by fans or players. Teams can be fined. Sometimes teams even have to play games without fans in the stadium.

Sepp Blatter is the president of soccer's world governing body. In 2013, he spoke out for tougher penalties for racism. He suggested that leagues should go so far as to dock points in the standings from teams that allow racism in their stands.

"The entire world fights against racism and discrimination," Blatter said. "[Soccer] is part of the world's society. We unite more than 300 million people around the world and should set an example. Without serious sanctions, nothing will ever change."

## CHAPTER 3

The 1999 Women's World Cup, won by the host team, the United States, proved that there could be great mainstream interest in women's team sports. ▶

# NO GIRLS ALLOWED

Men have always been the leaders in sports. Throughout history, men founded most sports. Most of the participants in those sports were men. And most of the people running the sports were men. So it is no surprise that men's sports tend to be more popular than women's sports. But women's sports are catching up.

Men's sports have been a major part of society for generations. People have grown up watching baseball since the mid-1800s. Women's sports only began to grow rapidly around the 1970s. Before then, women were sometimes barred from playing. Other times they were severely limited. This sexism was simply part of the culture.

For many years, people did not want to see women athletes. Sports were seen as an activity for men. Women were not supposed to swear or be aggressive. They were supposed to hide their bodies behind conservative clothing. Some people also claimed sports could be harmful to women. They worried that sports could hurt women's bodies, which they believed were more fragile than men's. Even worse, they worried sports could make women unable to have children.

Some women in the United States began to challenge these sexist beliefs by the late 1890s. The first women's track-and-field meet was held in 1895 at Vassar College in New York. But the event had to be largely private to avoid negative attention. The meet official was the only man allowed to attend.

Women's sports slowly grew over the next several years. The beginning of the modern Olympic Games in 1896 was a milestone for all sports. But the Olympics have been particularly important for women's sports. Men have always had many opportunities to play sports at a high level. For women, the Olympic Games have been the one constant world-class competition.

Yet women have also faced many challenges within the Olympics— some that still continue. The first obstacle to overcome was participation. A Frenchman, Pierre de Fredy, the Baron de Coubertin, founded the modern Olympics. He wanted to maintain many of the traditions from the ancient Greek Olympics. One of those traditions was that participation was limited to men.

The IOC barred women from the first Olympic Games, in 1896. The IOC relaxed its ban after that. In the 1900 Games, women competed in tennis and golf. More women's sports were added to the Games that followed. However, the women's program was always much smaller than the men's program. And women generally were limited to sports that were less physically demanding.

Track and field has always been one of the most popular sports at the Olympics. But the battle for women's inclusion in track and field has been long. Women's track and field was first allowed at the 1928 Games. Even then, only five women's events were offered. For the men, there were 22 track-and-field events.

The longest women's running event was 800 meters. Afterward, the runners appeared exhausted. They were sweating. All of that is considered normal today. But in 1928 it caused an international sensation. Afterward,

## CHASING EQUALITY

The women's track-and-field program has slowly grown at the Olympic Games. Since 2008, men compete in 24 events to 23 for the women. Some of the events differ slightly. Women run the 100-meter hurdles while men run 110-meter hurdles, for example. But only men compete in the 50-km race walk. Other sports are slowly catching up as well. Men's boxing has been part of the Olympics since 1904. A women's boxing competition was added in 2012. However, there were 10 men's weight classes to only 3 women's weight classes. With less history, women's boxing is less established than men's boxing. The same is true for many sports. Women's opportunities in the Olympics and other sporting events are expected to grow as participation continues to rise.

▲ Jackie Joyner-Kersee, the 1988 and 1992 Olympic decathlon champion, was one of the first women's sports stars of the Title IX generation.

the IOC cut the race out of the Olympic program. From 1932 until 1960, the longest women's race in the Olympics was 200 meters.

## TITLE IX

By the 1970s, women's rights had become a major issue. Women wanted equality in all areas. That included equality for girls and women in sports. Those efforts got a major boost in 1972. That year President Richard Nixon signed a law called Title IX. The law prohibited sex discrimination in federally funded educational institutions.

Title IX was written to give equality to women in all areas of public education. However, its lasting legacy has been its impact on sports. Federal money had long gone to support boys' sports in schools and colleges. Title IX said equal money had to be spent on girls' sports.

School sports had existed for some girls before Title IX. However, the funding and organization of girls' sports paled in comparison to that of boys' sports. After Title IX, many schools across the country began spending money on girls' sports for the first time.

This was a landmark change for women's sports. Suddenly high schools and colleges around the country began fielding more women's teams. That investment paid off in major ways. According to a 2012 Associated Press story, fewer than 300,000 high school girls played sports before Title IX. In 2012, the number had jumped to 3 million. Meanwhile, the United States became an international power in women's sports such as basketball, soccer, and ice hockey.

Participation rose with Title IX. Soon the higher levels of women's sports became more sophisticated too. The National

## TITLE IX OPPONENTS

In 1979, a new interpretation of Title IX created a three-part test of which schools had to meet one. According to a *New York Times* opinion story, the three parts are: "that the number of athletes from each sex be roughly equivalent to the number of students enrolled; that colleges demonstrate a commitment to adding women's sports; and that they prove that the athletic interests of female students are effectively accommodated." However, some people disagree with this interpretation. They believe that requiring equal numbers of men and women leads to discrimination against men's sports. Some schools have cited Title IX as a reason to cut men's sports teams.

Collegiate Athletic Association (NCAA) had long administered men's college sports. However, the NCAA long did not allow women. So other organizations oversaw women's sports. The NCAA removed its ban on women in 1973. In 1981, the NCAA officially took over governance of all college women's sports. That helped foster rapid growth. In 2012–13, the NCAA held 44 national championships for women's sports. It had 42 for men's sports and three co-ed national championships.

Women's sports got a boost in other countries during the 1970s as well. Soccer is the world's most popular sport. The modern rules were invented in England. That country has always been a leader in men's soccer. But the sport's organizers banned women from playing the sport in 1921. They claimed soccer was "quite unsuitable for females and ought not to be encouraged." Other countries made similar rulings. The English ban was lifted in 1971. West Germany lifted its ban one year earlier. Brazil did not lift its ban until 1979.

Women's soccer took off soon after. The Women's World Cup debuted in 1991. Women's soccer was added to the Olympic

## LOCKER ROOM ACCESS

As long as there have been sports, there have been people eager to read and write about sports. For decades sportswriters were all men. But as women earned more opportunities in the workforce in the 1970s, some women became sportswriters. This created a problem. Sportswriters usually interview athletes in locker rooms. And most teams barred women from entering men's locker rooms. They allowed women to do interviews outside the locker rooms. However, the access there was very limited compared to inside the locker room. The unequal access prevented the female writers from doing their job. That began to change in 1977. That year Time Inc. sued Major League Baseball (MLB) to get access for a female *Sports Illustrated* reporter. The other major sports leagues eventually followed.

Games in 1996. Both competitions have since grown into major events. And the Women's World Cup planned to expand from 16 teams to 24 in 2015. Meanwhile, professional leagues exist in the United States and other countries, mostly in Europe.

Other women's sports have also grown to become major spectator sports. Women's volleyball debuted in the Olympic Games in 1964. Women's basketball followed in 1976. In 1996, the Women's National Basketball Association (WNBA) began play. Other professional women's sports leagues had existed in the past, but none lasted. The WNBA survived early struggles to break that trend. In 2013, the league had 12 teams spread across the country. The WNBA relied heavily on the NBA for support in its early years. But in 2013, 6 of the 12 WNBA teams were independently owned.

Individual women's sports have seen progress as well. Women have long competed in tennis's four Grand Slam events. They are the Australian Open, French Open, US Open, and Wimbledon. The US Open began offering equal prize money to the men's and women's singles champion in 1973. When Wimbledon did the same in 2007, all four Grand Slams had equal prize money.

The efforts to create stable women's sports leagues have had setbacks, though. Many women's professional leagues have tried and failed. Usually they ran out of money. The National Women's Soccer

League debuted in the United States in 2013. It was the third attempt at a professional women's soccer league in the country in 12 years.

# LOOKING FORWARD

The year 2012 proved to be a big one for women's sports. For one, it was the fortieth anniversary of Title IX. Various celebrations and news articles celebrated the growth in women's sports after that.

Women also shined at that summer's Olympic Games in London. That year's US Olympic Team had more female athletes than men. That had never happened before. And US women won 58 of Team USA's 104 medals.

The 2012 Olympics were also the first in which each country sent at least one female athlete. In fact, women made up 44 percent of all Olympians in 2012. In 1984, women made up just 24 percent of Olympians.

## STILL FIGHTING TODAY

Men have been ski jumping at the Olympic Winter Games since 1924. However, women ski jumpers were not allowed for many years. In 2010, women skiers were allowed to test the Olympic course for the men. But the women were not allowed to ski jump for a medal. Women's ski jumping was officially added for the 2014 Olympic Winter Games in Sochi, Russia.

The addition of ski jumping was a big step forward, but it still did not signal full equality. The Nordic combined event includes both ski jumping and cross-country skiing. Women can now do both at the Winter Games. But the combined event involves two jumps on a large hill. One is with a team of four and the other is an individual jump. The current IOC rules do not permit women to jump on the large hill, either as an individual competitor or as part of a team.

▲ Members of the 2012 US women's soccer team stand on the podium with their gold medals at the London Olympic Games.

For women's sports advocates, there is still much work to be done. In some countries, women are still banned or shunned from playing sports. This is particularly true in the Middle East. In addition, male athletes around the world are often treated better than female athletes. For example, Japan's men's soccer team flew in business class to England for the 2012 Olympics. Meanwhile, the women, who ended up winning a silver medal, had to sit in coach on the same flight.

Women have made great advances in sports since the 1970s. Participation has skyrocketed since Title IX and similar laws in other countries. World championship and professional opportunities exist in many women's sports. But women's sports leaders know there is more work to be done. Groups such as the Women's Sports Foundation (WSF) are working to ensure the push toward equality continues. This includes getting more women into coaching, refereeing, administration, and other roles within sports.

## CHAPTER 4

Dr. Ludwig Guttmann founded what would become the Paralympic Games when he held the Stoke Mandeville Games in 1948. ▶

# OVERCOMING DISABILITIES

Some disabilities are physical. Others are mental or emotional. And for a long time, people who had disabilities were ignored in the sports world. The focus was on what the person with disabilities could not do, not what they could.

The Paralympic movement began during and after World War II. It has played a major role in changing that approach to disabilities. Similar to other wars, there were many soldiers who came home injured from World War II. In 1944, the English government asked Dr. Ludwig Guttmann to help some of these wounded soldiers. He started the Spinal Injuries Unit at the Stoke Mandeville military hospital.

At the time, most people who had spinal injuries did not recover. Many died less than a year after the injury. Guttmann had new ideas about how to help these wounded soldiers. He used sports to help them recover. These recovering soldiers' early games looked similar to polo and hockey put together. Instead of a polo horse, the soldiers rode a wheelchair. Just as in polo, the players chased the ball to hit it with a long stick.

Wheelchair polo was such a success that the hospital added more sports to the program. The soldiers started playing wheelchair basketball. Then Guttmann added archery to the soldiers' exercises. Archery became a popular sport at the hospital. The wounded soldiers who participated were paralyzed below the waist. They could not walk. But if they exercised, they could develop their upper body strength. Shooting a bow and arrow improves upper body strength.

The Olympic Games came to England in 1948. That gave Guttmann an idea. On the day of the 1948 Opening Ceremony in London, the doctor's soldiers had their own competition. Fourteen men and two women had an archery competition at the Stoke Mandeville hospital. All of these wounded soldiers competed in their wheelchairs. It was the first competition for wheelchair athletes. They called it the Stoke Mandeville Games.

Four years later, it was time for the next Olympic Games. The 1952 Olympic Games were in Helsinki, Finland. The hospital decided to have another competition, too. And this time wounded soldiers

from the Netherlands came to the hospital to compete. That made
their competition international. It was now the International Stoke
Mandeville Games.

## THE PARALYMPIC GAMES

The 1960 Olympic Games were held in Rome, Italy. A group of wheelchair
athletes held a competition there, too. These wheelchair games were
called the "Parallel" Olympics, or Paralympic Games. The word "para"
means beside.

The Paralympic Games took off from there. Four hundred athletes
from 23 countries came to compete in Rome. Four summers later, they did
it again. Both the Olympics and Paralympics continued every four years
after that. But they were often held in different cities.

That changed with the 1988 Summer Games and the 1992 Winter Games. Now the IOC and the IPC have an agreement. Host cities must host both the Olympics and Paralympics. Both events use many of the same venues. The agreement has helped raise the visibility of the Paralympics. That has led to increased opportunities.

The Paralympic Games were originally limited to those with spinal injuries. But the International Sports Organization for the Disabled (ISOD) wanted all of its members to play in the games. In 1976, two big changes were made. First, a winter competition was added. That meant there would be both winter and summer competitions, just like the Olympic Games.

## SPORTS FOR THE DISABLED

Sports for the disabled began with former soldiers. But soldiers were not the only disabled people who wanted to play sports. After the second Paralympic Games, in 1964, a group of former soldiers set up a new committee. They wanted to study the problems of sports for the disabled. This study resulted in a new group, the ISOD. The ISOD decided to create opportunities for those who could not compete in the Paralympic Games. So it welcomed athletes with cerebral palsy, amputations, paraplegia, and/or visual impairments.

The second big change was the addition of other athletes with disabilities. In 1976, athletes with amputations or visual impairments were allowed to compete. Four years later, athletes with cerebral palsy were added.

The ISOD continued to lobby for all of its members to have access to sports competition. Four years later, in 1984, another category was added. It was called "the others." It was for members who did not fit into the other four categories.

The sixth, and final, category of athletes was added to the games in 1996. This category was for athletes with an intellectual disability (ID). However, members of the Spanish basketball team were found to be faking their IDs at the 2000 Paralympics. The IPC kept this category closed for many years. It was not reopened until the IPC found a way to test athletes in this category. At the 2012 London Paralympic Games, the ID category was reopened for three sports: track and field, swimming, and table tennis.

## THE SPECIAL OLYMPICS

The Paralympics are not the only games for people with IDs. The Special Olympics is also for people with IDs. Eunice Kennedy Shriver, a sister of US President John F. Kennedy, started the Special Olympics. She did so after growing up playing sports with her older sister, Rosemary, who had an ID.

In 1968, the first International Special Olympics Summer Games were held at Soldier Field in Chicago. One thousand people with IDs from the United States and Canada competed in track and field and swimming. In 1977, winter games were added. The first International Special Olympics Winter Games took place in Steamboat Springs, Colorado. More than 500 athletes competed in skiing and ice skating events.

As time went by, countries all around the world changed laws and practices for people with IDs. Then they sent their athletes to the Special Olympics. Today, more than 3 million Special Olympic athletes train year-round in the United States and 180 other countries.

In 2008, *Sports Illustrated* gave its first Sportsman of the Year Legacy Award to Eunice Kennedy Shriver. It was the fortieth anniversary of the first Special Olympics. After announcing the award, writer Jack McCallum gave *Sports Illustrated* readers some background:

> But to say that the lot of people with intellectual disabilities has improved because of Special Olympics is so grossly understated as to be meaningless. Shriver's movement did nothing less than release an entire population from a prison of ignorance and misunderstanding. It did something else, too—create a cathartic covenant between competitor and fan that is unlike anything else in sport. You watch and what you see is nothing less than a transformation, the passage of someone who has been labeled unfortunate, handicapped, disabled, or challenged to something else: athlete.

Source: Jack McCallum. "Small Steps, Great Strides." SI Vault. Time Inc., 8 Dec. 2008. Web. 27 June 2013.

## What's the Big Idea?

Eunice Kennedy Shriver wanted to see what people with IDs could do, not what they could not do. The work she did began in her own backyard, but it spread around the world. Why was this work important? How did it change lives?

## CONTINUING BATTLE

Opportunities for those with disabilities have grown dramatically over the years. Those opportunities have not always come easy, though.

Tatyana McFadden was born with a condition that left her paralyzed below the waist. That means she can never run in a track meet. But few can compete with her in a wheelchair race around the track. At the 2012 Paralympics, McFadden won gold medals in the 400-, 800-, and 1,500-meter races. She also won a bronze medal in the 100 meters. Plus she had claimed five major marathon victories through July 2013.

McFadden had to fight for her opportunity to compete in sports, though. She grew up in Maryland. McFadden was competitive. But she was forced to race in a separate wheelchair division at track-and-field meets. That meant she was often racing against herself. So she sued the state. Eventually she earned the right to compete alongside athletes without disabilities.

"All I wanted to do in high school was get involved in sport and be on par with my peers," she said. "That was a very tough battle, but it was worth fighting for because it gave other people the opportunity to do sport."

## A MORE INCLUSIVE FUTURE?

Disabled sports are organized from the grassroots to the Paralympic level in the United States. Over the years, more opportunities have arisen for youth athletes in schools and local clubs. But similar opportunities are not available in other countries. In 2012, more than 4,000 athletes from 163 countries competed at the Paralympic Games in London. But officials noted that many poorer countries were underrepresented. Charles Narh Teye is a powerlifter from Ghana who competed in London. He shared some of the difficulties disabled athletes face in his country:

*The most difficult thing was that in school people thought that if you were physically challenged it could easily be transferred to other people. People wouldn't sit near me. They thought that if my prosthetics should touch them they would have an amputation. I had to sit at the back of the class with the teachers. I couldn't play, because no one wanted to come close to me. I was lonely all the time.*

*It was very difficult.*

Disabilities are unique and wide-ranging. And with the rise in disabled sports, questions have risen about how to categorize competitions. Swimmer Victoria Arlen was one of the stars of Team USA at the 2012 Paralympics. However, she was barred from competing in the next year's world championships. The IPC determined her paralysis was not permanent enough.

////////////////////////

## MURDERBALL

**Wheelchair rugby was added to the Paralympic Games in 2000. The sport gained a new level of fame after the 2005 documentary *Murderball*. The Oscar-nominated film followed the US and Canadian teams leading into the 2004 Paralympics. It showed a side to disabled sports that many people had never seen before. The athletes were intense, physical, and ultracompetitive. In 2012, *Time* magazine called wheelchair rugby "the hottest ticket" of the Paralympic Games after tickets sold out in three days. *Time* credited the sport's popularity to the 2005 film.**

//////////////////////////////////////////////

Australia's Ryley Batt, *right*, battles for the ▲
ball with Canada's Zak Madell during the 2012
Paralympics wheelchair rugby gold-medal game.

The controversy drew a lot of attention. Some people believed it made the IPC look bad. But IPC president Phillip Craven was not one of them. He believed that controversies such as the one surrounding the decision about Arlen showed that disabled sports were being taken seriously. People now look at Paralympic sports as a true form of competition, not a form of charity.

"We celebrated 20 years of the International Paralympic Committee in 2009 and I said at the end of my speech that the biggest achievement of the past eight or nine years has been the transformation of the Paralympic movement from a disability with a big 'D' sports movement to an international sports movement," he said.

## CHAPTER 5

# COMING OUT

On April 29, 2013, Jason Collins told *Sports Illustrated*, "I'm a 34-year-old NBA center. I'm black. And I'm gay." His face appeared on the cover of the magazine with the headline, "The Gay Athlete." The cover also had this quote from the article.

"I didn't set out to be the first openly gay athlete playing in a major American team sport," he said. "But since I am, I'm happy to start the conversation."

The term "sexual orientation" describes what sex a person is physically and emotionally attracted to. Some people are heterosexual. That means they are attracted to individuals of the opposite sex. Some people are

homosexual. They are attracted to individuals of the same sex. Bisexual people are attracted to both individuals of the same and opposite sex. Gender and sex are defined differently. Gender might appear to be easy to identify. A person is born as a male or a female. But which sex a person identifies with does not always match the person's sex at birth. People who identify and express themselves as the opposite sex are called transgender.

LGBT people have faced discrimination and oppression for centuries. This has sometimes been violent. People often oppose LGBT orientations for religious or moral reasons. Only one man and one woman can conceive a child. So some people believe homosexuality, bisexuality, and transgender orientations are unnatural. Up until the 1970s, the American Psychiatric Association (APA) classified homosexuality as a mental illness.

Because of these perceptions, many LGBT people were forced to keep their sexuality or gender identity a secret. If not, they faced the potential loss of jobs, housing, or schooling options.

Attitudes about LGBT orientations began to change in the 1960s. People started to question traditional beliefs about sexuality. One of the results was more

## SUPPORT FOR JASON COLLINS

The reaction to Jason Collins's announcement was largely positive. When Collins came out, President Barack Obama called to express his support. First Lady Michelle Obama showed her support on Twitter. Collins's fellow athletes also used Twitter to reach out. Chris Kluwe of the Minnesota Vikings wrote: "Living proof that your sexuality has nothing to do with your athletic ability." Then he shared the *Sports Illustrated* link so his own fans could read the article.

people opening up about their sexuality. The scientific study of sexual orientation began to change as well. The APA's decision to stop considering homosexuality a mental illness was a major milestone. However, there remains no consensus among experts as to why sexual orientation differs between people. And many people today still have religious or moral opposition to these sexual orientations.

Many experts believe that fear of persecution has long kept most LGBT professional athletes from revealing their sexual orientation. In 1975, NFL running back Dave Kopay was the first athlete from a major professional team sport to come out. But he shared that news three years after he retired.

## TRANSGENDER ATHLETES

In 2013, California passed a law that protected the rights of transgender students from kindergarten through high school. Among other things, the law gave transgender students the right to pick which team they play for, boys or girls. Other states and sports organizations, including the NCAA, have made similar rules. But the question of transgender rights in sports remains controversial. In 2013, mixed martial artist Fallon Fox said she had been born a man. She underwent surgery and took hormones to alter her sex. Her transition met the criteria set up by the Association of Boxing Commissions to compete in the women's division. Many said they were uncomfortable with Fox fighting other women, though. "It's an advantage," fellow fighter Ronda Rousey said. "I don't think it's fair."

## "OUTED"

Billie Jean King was by any definition a women's tennis superstar. The Californian won her first Grand Slam singles title at Wimbledon in 1966. Over the next 9 years she won 11 more Grand Slam singles titles. She also won 16 Grand Slam women's doubles titles and 11 mixed doubles titles

over her career. She was also a public supporter for women's rights. King was one of the most famous female athletes of her time.

In 1981, King's stardom fell. She was married to a man named Larry King. However, a lawsuit revealed that Billie Jean King had formerly had a relationship with another woman. The public reaction was swift. In the next 24 hours, she lost all of her endorsements.

"It was very clear they dropped me because of the sexuality issue," said King, who claims she lost millions of dollars over the next several years. Athletes in those days did not make as much money as they do today. Endorsements were a vital part of their income.

King later revealed that she was bisexual. But she said she had not been ready to come out. Instead, somebody else had made that decision for her.

King was not alone, however. Martina Navratilova took King's place as the greatest women's tennis player in the late 1970s. Over her career Navratilova would win 18 Grand Slam singles titles, 31 Grand Slam doubles titles, and 10 Grand Slam mixed doubles titles. Many consider her to be the greatest tennis player ever. And in 1981, Navratilova came out as a lesbian. She said she did not want to hide who she was out of fear of being discriminated against.

"I've always had this outrage against being told how to live, what to say, how to act, what to do, when to do it," she once said.

Like King, Navratilova likely lost millions of dollars in endorsements after her announcement. But unlike King, Navratilova was still in the prime of her career when she came out. Navratilova gracefully dealt with homophobia during her career. Many credit her with paving the way for future LGBT athletes to feel comfortable coming out.

"Martina was the first legitimate superstar who literally came out while she was a superstar," said Donna Lopiano, executive director of the WSF. "She exploded the barrier by putting it on the table. She basically

▲ **Baylor University's Brittney Griner (42) was one of the most dominant women's college basketball players ever.**

said, 'This part of my life doesn't have anything to do with me as a tennis player. Judge me for who I am.'"

## CHANGING PERSPECTIVES

Several more athletes have come out publicly since King and Navratilova. Some of them were high-profile females, such as basketball player Brittney Griner and soccer player Megan Rapinoe. Famous male athletes have come out too. Among them were legendary Olympic diver Greg Louganis and figure skater Johnny Weir. However, Collins's announcement in April 2013 proved to be a major milestone. People had seen what happened when King came out. Many believe other LGBT athletes never came out because they feared similar reactions. Then Collins came out during the NBA offseason. Soon after, in May, soccer player Robbie Rogers joined the Los Angeles Galaxy. That made Rogers the first openly gay player in a major US men's team sport.

Attitudes about LGBT orientations were already changing by then. Through August 2013, 13 states and Washington DC had legalized gay marriage. Rogers entered his first MLS game as a substitute. The crowd of 24,811 gave him a standing ovation.

"I am proud to be part of a sport that has been so supportive of [Rogers]," MLS commissioner Don Garber tweeted. "I admire his courage and hope he stays involved in the game."

Other US leagues have shown similar support for the LGBT community. NFL commissioner Roger Goodell said he thinks a gay player "will be accepted" in the league. MLB announced policies in 2013. New York Attorney General Eric Schneiderman said they will send "a message that no professional athlete—professional or amateur—should have to sit on the sidelines or hide out of fear of being mistreated because of their sexual orientation." In the NBA, commissioner David Stern and star player Kobe Bryant both spoke in support of Collins after his decision. In fact, many said they believed that Collins and Rogers would actually get more endorsement deals because of their announcements.

## INTERNATIONAL LAWS

The year 2013 began a golden era of sports in Russia. The track-and-field world championships were held that year in Moscow. The Olympic Winter Games were scheduled for 2014 in Sochi. And the 2018 soccer World Cup was set to take place there as well. However, Russia passed a vague new law in June 2013 that could send people to jail for promoting homosexuality. Many in the international community were outraged. Some even called for the US Olympic Team to boycott the 2014 Olympics. Many others reject that idea. They say athletes can be more effective by speaking and acting out against the law. US 800-meter runner Nick Symmonds was one of the first to do so. He won a silver medal at the 2013 world championships. Then he dedicated his medal to his gay and lesbian friends. "Whether you're gay, straight, black, white, we all deserve the same rights," he said.

## NOT ALL OPEN

Still, many believe that there are more LGBT athletes who are not comfortable coming out. There could be several reasons for this. For one, some athletes might believe their sexual orientation is private and does not need to be made public. There are also still concerns about how a player will be accepted. For all of the supportive talk from commissioners and players, antigay slurs and actions still occur.

In January 2013, San Francisco 49ers cornerback Chris Culliver was asked if there were gay players on his team. "No, we don't got no gay people on the team," he replied. "They gotta get up out of here if they do." Culliver later apologized for the comments. He said, "Those discriminating feelings are truly not in my heart." However, his comments highlighted the macho locker room culture that exists in many men's sports. Toronto Blue Jays pitcher Brandon Morrow had a similar view. He said he would be okay with a gay player. However, he believes the sports culture might lead to uncomfortable situations.

Jason Collins, *center*, marches in the Boston Pride ▲
Parade in 2013.

"I think [being an openly gay player] would be extremely difficult because of the culture," Morrow said. "Not that I think there's a lot of anti-gay sentiment around, it's just that masculine feel in the clubhouse."

Sports have made great gains in equality issues over the years. The days when athletes could be barred from competing because of their skin color or their sex are over. And opportunities for traditionally discriminated groups, such as LGBT athletes and disabled athletes, have greatly improved. However, those who have experienced discrimination know that the battle for equality in sports is not complete.

"When gay rights becomes a non-issue, the LGBT community can exhale," King said.

# DISCUSSION QUESTIONS

## Say What?

The world of sports has its own vocabulary. Find five words in this book that you have never heard before. Use a dictionary to find out what they mean. Then write the meanings in your own words and use each word in a new sentence.

## Tell the Tale

In Chapter Four, the book tells of how Dr. Ludwig Guttmann started a new unit at the military hospital. Write a 200-word narrative describing what happened there. Begin with the problem the doctor faced, and then share specific examples of the steps he took to resolve this problem.

## Surprise Me

This book discussed society's reaction to discovering the sexual identity of some professional athletes. In 1981, the athletes lost all of their endorsements. In 2013, many of these athletes received support. Which reaction did you find more surprising? Write a paragraph explaining why.

## Dig Deeper

For a case to be heard by the Supreme Court, it has to be heard in the lower courts first. Why was Title IX challenged in the courts? Do some research to find out and then make your own judicial ruling. Do you think that the law should have been upheld? Just like a judge, cite specific examples to back up your statement.

**amateur**

A person who plays a sport without being paid.

**bias**

A preconceived opinion about a subject that makes it hard to fairly judge the subject.

**discrimination**

Making a distinction for or against a person based on the group that person belongs to or on that person's characteristics or traits.

**equality**

The state of being equal, or alike; evenly proportioned or balanced.

**grassroots**

Organization that begins at the lowest, or most basic, level.

**homophobia**

A hatred or fear of homosexuality.

**integration**

To combine schools, teams, and other things previously segregated by race into one unified system.

**prejudice**

An unfavorable opinion or feeling formed beforehand or without knowledge, thought, or reason.

**prosthetic**

A device that substitutes for a missing or defective part of the body.

**rehabilitation**

A process of restoring normal life.

**sanctions**

Penalties.

**segregation**

To separate or set apart from others or from the main body or group.

## SELECTED BIBLIOGRAPHY

Collins, Jason, with Franz Lidz. "Why NBA Center Jason Collins is Coming Out Now." *Sports Illustrated*. Time, 29 April 2013. Web. 11 July 2013.

Ford, Bonnie D. "Women's Ski Jump OK'd, but Battle Not Over." *ESPN*. ESPN Internet Ventures, 6 April 2011. Web. 11 July 2013.

Middlehurst-Schwartz, Michael. "Robbie Rogers Makes History as MLS' First Openly Gay Player." *USA TODAY Sports*. Gannett, 27 May 2013. Web. 11 July 2013.

Thomas, Katie. "After Long Fight for Inclusion, Women's Ski Jumping Gains Olympic Status." *The New York Times*. New York Times, 6 April 2011. Web. 11 July 2013.

Thomas, Katie. "Women Can Only Test the Hills." *The New York Times*. New York Times, 21 Feb. 2010. Web. 11 July 2013.

## FURTHER READINGS

Bobrick, Benson. *A Passion for Victory: The Story of the Olympics in Ancient and Early Modern Times*. New York: Knopf, 2012. Print.

Schilling, Vincent. *Native Athletes in Action!*. Summertown, TN: 7th Generation, 2007. Print.

Smith, Charles R. *Stars in the Shadows: The Negro League All-Star Game of 1934*. New York: Atheneum, 2012. Print.

Stout, Glenn. *Yes, She Can! Women's Sports Pioneers*. New York: Houghton/ Sandpiper, 2011. Print.

## WEB SITES

To learn more about equality in sports, visit ABDO Publishing Company online at **www.abdopublishing.com**. Web sites about equality in sports are featured on our Book Links page. These links are routinely monitored and updated to provide the most current information available.

## PLACES TO VISIT

**Naismith Memorial Basketball Hall of Fame**

1000 Hall of Fame Avenue
Springfield, MA 01105
877-4HOOPLA
**www.hoophall.com**

The Naismith Memorial Basketball Hall of Fame is home to nearly 300 inductees and more than 40,000 square feet of basketball history.

**National Baseball Hall of Fame and Museum**

25 Main Street
Cooperstown, NY 13326
888-HALL-OF-FAME (888-425-5633)
**www.baseballhall.org**

The National Baseball Hall of Fame and Museum collections feature almost 40,000 three-dimensional items, three million books and documents, and 500,000 photographs.

# INDEX

AIDS, 7
apartheid, 6–7
Arlen, Victoria, 48–49
Ashe, Arthur, 4–8

banning players, 9, 10, 19, 31, 34, 37, 38, 59
baseball, 9, 16–21, 22, 23, 28, 34
Blatter, Sepp, 26
boxing, 23, 31, 53

Cassidy, Josh, 14
Collins, Jason, 50, 52, 56–57

football, 9, 23, 25

hockey, 24–25, 33, 42

integrating sports, 18, 21, 23–24
intellectual disabilities, 45, 46
International Olympic Committee, 7, 31–32, 37, 44
International Paralympic Committee, 14, 44, 45, 48–49
international sports, 6–7, 14, 25–26, 31, 43–44, 45, 49, 58

King, Billie Jean, 53–57, 59

LGBT rights, 10–11, 13, 53
Major League Baseball, 34, 57
McFadden, Tatyana, 47
Murderball, 48
National Basketball Association, 11–13, 23, 35, 50, 57
National Collegiate Athletic Association, 33–34, 53
National Football League, 23, 53, 57
National Hockey League, 24–25
Navratilova, Martina, 55–56
Negro Leagues, 20

Olympic Games, 6–7, 10, 14, 19, 23, 30–32, 34–35, 37–39, 42–44, 56, 58
Owens, Jesse, 19, 23

Paralympic Games, 14–15, 40, 43–45, 47–49

racism, 6–7, 8–9, 16–21, 23–26
Rickey, Branch, 16, 18, 20–21, 23
Robinson, Jackie, 18, 21, 22, 23, 25
Rogers, Robbie, 11, 57

segregation, 6, 9, 16, 19–20, 23
sexism, 9–10, 28–33
Shriver, Eunice Kennedy, 45, 46
ski jumping, 37
soccer, 7, 11, 25–26, 33–37, 38–39, 56–57, 58
South Africa, 6–7
Special Olympics, 45, 46
stereotypes, 9, 25
Stoke Mandeville Games, 40–43

tennis, 4–7, 31, 35, 53–56
Title IX, 32–33, 37, 39
track and field, 19, 31, 45, 47, 58
transgender athletes, 10, 52, 53

Ward, Joel, 24–25
Warrior Games, 15
wheelchair sports, 14, 42, 43, 47, 48
Women's National Basketball Association, 35
Women's Sports Foundation, 39, 55
World Cup, 7, 34–35, 58

## ABOUT THE AUTHOR

Tracy Miller is a former elementary and middle school English teacher. A lifelong sports fan, she played softball, skateboarded, and cycled in middle school. Today, she swims, jogs, and practices yoga. Miller is the author of dozens of books for young readers.